# The Five Stages
## *of*
# Quitting Farming

John William Kulm

# The Five Stages of Quitting Farming
a *gazoobi tales* book

For information address:
gazoobi tales,
p.o.b. 12651
Everett, WA 98206

ISBN 0-9679364-8-9

Library of Congress Control Number:   2002107717

book design by Thomas Hubbard
10 9 8 7 6 5 4 3 2 1

*For my parents — real farmers.*

# INTRODUCTION
## by Jens Lund, Ph.D.

In the last few decades traditional industries of the American West, such as ranching, farming, logging and mining, have suffered major setbacks. Some of the reversals are the consequence of foreign competition. Others are due to changes in consumers' market preferences. Still others are the result of environmental policies, in some cases necessary and in others probably not. A few of our ranchers, farmers and loggers have taken to writing poems addressing these issues. Some might call this exercise "therapy." Others might call it "protest." Perhaps it is a little of both.

In this volume, ex-farmer John Kulm looks back at his family's history of farming—four generations in the Pacific Northwest and an unknown number of generations in Russia and Germany before that—and asks himself, his family and our society, "What went wrong?" The reader may ask, "Why does he choose poetry?" His motivations are his own, but in choosing verse he carries on a long tradition of composing poems about farming, a tradition at least as old as Vergil's first century B.C. *Georgics*.

Although John writes mostly in the free-verse style of the late twentieth century, his work continues the much older American traditions of the rural "occasion poet" and the occupational poet. Well into the late twentieth century, farm journals and local newspapers in farm country used poetry for filler. Many rural communities had their own "occasion poet," who could be counted on to compose verses for a funeral, a graduation, or a patriotic occasion. Especially in farm journals, these rustic poets evoked images of agriculture and rural life, often with a nostalgic cast.

Before the days of the phonograph and radio, people working in isolated locales made their own entertainment. Among them were cowboys, farmers, fishermen, loggers, miners and sailors. The challenges and rewards of these people's difficult, dangerous work were often best expressed in the form of folk poetry.

Cowboy poems first appeared in ranching trade periodicals and local newspapers of ranching areas. Published poems about ranch life became numerous during the 1870s. In the next decade, much of the West began to be homesteaded and the open cattle drives of the late 1860s and 1870s became a focus of nostalgia. This seems to have increased the composition and dissemination of cowboy poems, perhaps also by creating a class of more sedentary ranch-hands with access to the possibility of writing and distributing their expressions.

John Kulm was first exposed to cowboy poetry while doing standup comedy in Montana in 1985. He had been writing poetry, some of it about farm and ranch life, since childhood, but he had not yet shared any of it outside his family. In his words, "Reciting humorous cowboy poems was easy; it was like telling a joke, but sharing serious stuff with the public was riskier."

In 1993, the grunge scene in Seattle's nightclubs was in full swing. John was already a fixture of Northwest comedy clubs, reciting his humorous ranch verse wearing a cowboy hat and picking a five-string banjo. At a poetry slam in a Seattle bar, he heard angry and rowdy young poets get up in front of crowds and share their innermost feelings. "If they can do it, so can I," he thought, and he began inserting intermittent serious material into his club performances. This led to an invitation to perform at the 1994 Lollapalooza.

I met John at the Arts Northwest Conference in Tacoma, Washington in 1992. He was invited to perform at the National Cowboy Poetry Gathering at Elko, Nevada, in 1996. In 1997, I visited him at his home in Chinook. My job was to survey folk poets for New York City's City Lore, Inc., as they laid plans for an international People's Poetry Gathering in 1999. At that visit, John first shared with me his poems evoking the predicament of Western agriculture and they blew me away.

Since then, John has written lots more of this material. I have seen him thrill a New York City audience at the 2001 People's Poetry Gathering with heartfelt and lyrical tales of the trials and tribulations of the Western farmer trying to make it in a world where the cards are stacked against his success.

This volume brings some of John's best poems together in an autobiographical format and reveals the story of the farmer who can no longer farm. Read it and understand where our farmers have been and where they are going. Read it and ask yourself: "Where does the wheat in our bread, the beef in our burgers and the cotton in our drawers come from?" Read it and consider the men and women whose daily work has brought us these and the thousands of other products we have taken for granted.

# Contents

# The Five Stages of Quitting Farming

**M**y mom said to me, "I hope your book isn't too depressing. Farmers aren't like that. Farmers are optimists. Your father was always optimistic about things getting better." It's true that he seldom acted depressed or angry, but there were years when the stress made him carry antacid tablets in his pickup.

I'm not a farmer these days. If some of these poems don't sound optimistic, it's because I decided to write what was on my mind. If some of the poems sound angry or melancholy, it's because I wanted to express those things for the guys who are too optimistic to do that for themselves.

Our current agriculture recession is in its fifth year and ranks among the deepest in United States history. This is an economy where many farmers have been forced into a corner where they have only one option: give up.

Being forced to quit is a frustrating situation for entrepreneurs who once were praised for being the people who would feed the world. Today our nation's farmers struggle to compete with low prices of food imported from other countries, and the world uses technologies developed in the United States to feed us.

Leaving a farm is a kind of loss, similar to the loss of a loved one. Grieving over the loss of a career in farming involves a natural process.

Dr. Elisabeth Kubler-Ross traced five stages of grief for the dying as being (1) denial and isolation, (2) anger, (3) bargaining, (4) depression, and (5) acceptance. Dr. Erich Lindemann was the first person to suggest there are stages of grief, listing them as (1) somatic distress, (2) pre-occupation with the image of the deceased, (3) guilt, (4) hostile reactions, and (5) loss of patterns of conduct.

Other authors have similar lists. I think that the stages of grief are experienced differently by each person. This is a poetry book, not a treatise on psychology, and the categories are listed in the way I experienced them.

# Denial and Shock

The first stage of grieving is denial and shock. Farmers are good at living in denial. I remember applying for an operating loan with the Farm Service Agency. The balance sheet didn't look very positive so I just raised the price I expected to get for the apples and I raised the corn yield, and then the balance sheet looked better. I was making a lot of money. This is easier to do on a balance sheet than it is in the real world. If you think a balance sheet is the same as the real world, you may be living in denial.

I needed six tons of dry corn per acre. This isn't impossible on irrigated ground. I showed my dad a chart from the fertilizer company. It said we could get one ton of corn for every fifty pounds of nitrogen fertilizer we applied, so I was ordering three hundred pounds per acre so I could get six tons of corn. My dad grinned and said, "Why not put on nine hundred pounds and get eighteen ton?"

Shock may set in as your credit gets cut off at the seed company, the chemical company, the parts shop. Shock is your body's way of surviving the situations your mind gets you into. It's normal and healthy to go through a state of denial and shock. It isn't healthy to stay there forever.

If the bank's foreclosed on your land and the chemical companies lock their doors when they see you coming and you're still writing balance sheets, you may have remained in the stage of denial too long. You should think about scheduling a counseling session with your minister.

## The Price Will Come Back

"The price will come back," is what
      a cranberry grower told me.
When a man says the price will come back
don't you laugh at him and
don't you ask him something cynical like,
"What's gonna make it come back?
They grow cranberries in South America and
      they ship 'em to the supermarket in your town cheaper
      than you can grow 'em two miles from Safeway."
Just keep saying the price will come back,
      cranberry grower.
Say it until you believe it yourself.
The United States Department of Agriculture has
      a plan to cut production by 33 percent,
and maybe that'll bring the price back.
Just maybe if you can stop Argentina from
      sending 66 percent more over here.
And then the price will come back.
When a man's invested all his money and time and
      life and hope into the future of the
      price of a berry,
better be discrete about your wise-mouth remarks.
He bought that multi-million dollar white-elephant
      swampland over there:

environmental impact statements;

wetland protection policies.

Hard getting permission to turn another wetland

       into a berry bog.

It doesn't even matter because new varieties of

       cranberries are being genetically engineered to

       grow on dry land

       anywhere and everywhere:

Cranberries across the fruited plain

       from sea to shining sea.

But the price will come back.


The price will come back,

and the Brooklyn Dodgers will come back,

and Amelia Earhart will come back,

and Soviet Socialism will come back,

and the Salmon will come back,

and the wheat price will come back,

and the apple price will come back,

and the onion price will come back,

and no one knows the hour or the day but

Jesus Christ will come back.

Just keep saying it until you believe it yourself.

## An Irrigation Ditch

An irrigation ditch one mile long,
two thousand rows of corn,
three hundred siphon tubes spread out
  one in seven rows,
and eleven empty beer cans at the headgate.
A party here last night
and I wasn't invited.

Eighty-five degrees at seven-thirty a.m.,
four thousand two hundred steps up and back,
head hot, feet wet,
seeds of watergrass in the hair on my arms,
and one can of Bud Light spinning
  under the cold water pouring
  over a check in the ditch:
fugitive; escapee.

Noisy place:
water rushing; corn stalks rattle;
– pop – a beer can opens.

## A Shovel

Just give me one thing:
A double-aught shovel,
as sophisticated as Roy Clark in a Calvin Klein ad
pickin' and grinnin' his way across the bare-blazing
      belly-buttons of the anorexic
      too-cool-to-smile fashion toothpicks.
A shovel so fine I can feed the world
like a giant spoon scooping grain into the
      mouth of global consumerism.
Eat your vegetables you little complainer.

A shovel:
The kind those hat-wearing line dancers on
      The Nashville Network scowl at.
Garth Brooks wannabes, whining,
"A cowboy doesn't shovel dirt.
      I stay on my horse."
Stay on your horse then, singing your
      "git along little dogie" ditties.
I'll be doing the work and, hey,
      do you think I believe Charlie Goodnight and
      Bill Picket sang sing-alongs around the
      campfire while they pulled sand burs off of their
      saddle-sore buttockses?

A double-aught, heat tempered,
      made in the USA shovel:
Balanced so perfect I can throw it forty yards
      and sink its blade into a
      sod-covered ditch bank;
carry it along swinging it with the same intimacy
      as a drill sergeant has for his rifle
      *and* for his gun.
Not like one of your cheapo made-by-a-ten-cents-
      an-hour-third-world-nation-labor-force-multinational-
      corporation-shovel shovels.
Those two-for-ten-dollar backyard gardener shovels,
struggling against your grip as its screw-you
      angled blade fights for dominance
      against your will.


A double-aught shovel like a halberd in the hands
      of a foot soldier peasant
cursing the knights in shining armor riding their
      class-conscious quarter horses.
Tell me to choose my weapon.
I choose a double-aught, heat-tempered,
      made-in-the-USA shovel
heavy enough to work with and
      light enough to dance with;
moving with you like part of your arm, body,
      heart and soul shovel.

A double-aught shovel
tempered like a bell
          ringing in the hands of a Protestant heretic
          Augustinian monk, shouting,
"The priesthood is for everyone."
We are all priests of God.
God is not just speaking to the knights and the lords
          and the bishops and the pope.
God is in the dirt in the cracks of the hands
          of the worker
holding a double-aught, heat-tempered,
made-in-the-USA
shovel.

## Things I Recall

Six march side-by-side:
Mechanical planter units
on a tool bar.

Things I recall of my youth.
It wasn't so long ago.

Running through a field
to the man on a tractor.
Wave to the school bus.

Sensations my kids won't have;
I won't have with my children.

Stairs up to a tractor cab;
a/m f/m cassette,
air conditioning.

Practically lived in there.
Only a memory now.

Pull the string, open the bag:
Eighty-five pounds of corn seed
fills the pot.

Very different childhood.
Maybe all are different.

Fungicide for the seed.
More goes to the wind
than to the units.

"If I forget you, Jerusalem..."
No one cares about your memories.

Scent of sagebrush after the rain.
Scent of fungicide
on my fingers.

# Depression

There's a stage in the process of recovering from a loss when you'll travel through a land of depression. It might not help to know this, but you're not alone in that place. That place is filled with people who feel just like you, but you can't see them. The darkness is so thick in this land that you won't see anything except yourself and your own misery.

It's okay to live here for a little while, to get a handle on what's happened in your life. You won't be here forever, even if you might want to just lie in bed and never get up.

Darkness is always followed by daylight eventually. However, just so you'll know what to expect, there will be a time of depression and it's going to hurt.

## Next Year Country

Tradition
in our family goes way back
four generations, three traditions:
It was work and it was hope and
it was always disappointment.
Working hours, hoping next year
life would be a little better,
and we gave the land a name.
We call the farmland Next Year Country.

We love the hours before the sun is up,
in early morning mud and irrigation.
Father's back is sore from lifting, and
his knees are worn and tired.
Irrigation water is in his pant legs;
in his shirt sleeves
in the cold of early morning.
Love the taste of it around us.
Calves are playing in the pasture and
the shadows from the rising sun'll show
the corn is pushing up and peeking out;
the pinto beans are pushing up;
and the alfalfa's greening up;
the winter wheat is waking up.

And there's a promise and a hope in all the work:
May the prices all be up, and
may the yields all be up.


We come in for breakfast.
Mom has eggs and bacon, toast and
      fried potatoes waiting.
Dad is eating with a magazine in front of him, and
      aching in his shoulders, and
      the aching in his hands.
Mud across the floor for mom before we go.
My dad had dreams when he was younger of a
      ranch with Uncle Roy.
Uncle Roy who lost his son
and lost his own dreams when that happened.
Mom had dreams she never told us,
      and she put 'em off till next year.
Always next year in this country.
This is next year country here.


And it was work and it was hope and
it was always disappointment.
I don't care that I don't have a lot of education
'cause I love the hours before the sun is up
in early morning mud and irrigation,
with my back all sore from lifting,
and my knees all worn and tired.
Irrigation water in my boots and in my socks

and irrigation water in my pant legs;
in my shirt sleeves;
in the cold of early morning.
Love the taste of it around us.


We had dreams once of a good year.
May the prices and the yields
      both be up for once together.
Simple dreaming when I asked my dad,
"Where did we get that saying,
      'next year country'?"
He told me, "Your grandpa's father used to say it
      long before we both were born."
It's always been.
It's always this is next year country here.


Every day of every spring,
      in the early morning hours
calves are playing in the pasture and
the shadows from the rising sun'll show
the corn is pushing up and peeking out;
the pinto beans are pushing up;
and the alfalfa's greening up;
the winter wheat is waking up.
And there's a promise and a hope.
And there's promise... hope.

## A Thirty-three Horse Team

My grandfather had a team of thirty-three draft horses to pull the wheat harvester through the fields. When dad was five or six years old his job was to fill a bucket with rocks and hand it up to my grandpa who was driving the outfit so grandpa could pitch a rock at any of the horses who needed to shape up.

Heaving rocks at horses sounds a little cruel today. But they were just little stones and my grandpa understood those animals in a way, I'd guess, that's lost to most people. He had a bay saddle horse named Pat tied up behind the harvester to follow along in case they needed to make a trip back from the fields for anything.

A day for them was harnessing a thirty-three horse team in the morning and driving them out to the fields, feeding them and caring for them at night, along with putting up the harness lines at the end of the day. They'd find the time between to harvest endless rolling hills all blanketed with wheat to be hauled out in one-hundred-twenty pound bags loaded onto horse-drawn wagons they called header-boxes. One-hundred-degree days calling them to work.

This is something that I've never seen; never will see. One time I saw a hay rake pulled behind a two-horse team, but that's just a novelty. A thirty-three horse team is a spectacle; magnificent. Only Hollywood could recreate it anymore, maybe with computer graphics.

If I never see it, I'll be okay. Maybe my sons will be okay if they never see a three-point hitch behind a John Deere tractor sinking a gang of plowshares into the earth. Funny to think they'll grow up without a memory of moldboard plows, the same way I grew up without one time ever filling a bucket of rocks to hand up to the driver.

## Cemetery

There's a cemetery in this wheat field.
I don't know where.
Boxed up homesteaders hidden away.
I know there's a cemetery here:
long forgotten mothers, fathers, daughters, sons and
      hired men who never did mention their last names or
      where they were from.

The man who farms this land explained,
he said he didn't like driving his harvester
      around the headstones.
So he pulled the markers up and over on the
      south side of his shed
they're in a pile of marble; cast-off commemorations;
misplaced memorials; rocks of ages in the way;
stacked into irreverent irrelevance;
granite chipped from rock to ashes to ashes
      to dust to dust.

And he assures me, the dead don't care.
And I don't suppose they do care... very much.
They don't care.
Maybe they'd just as soon be

under an unmarked acreage
of an amber wave of grain
and a little bit productive for a change.


Scrubby dry-land farm there lucky to get an eighty
bushel yield to the acre on a good year.
And the dead don't care.
They don't care.
Generation after generation bury their dreams
along with the crop failures.
One sweep of the field cultivator and a family's
final resting-place is hidden away
under a fresh fall planting.
There's a cemetery here. I don't know where.
So have a grim respect for this hillside panorama;
ancestral seedbed;
crematorium of wheat;
Forest Lawn granary;
Arlington National stubble field;
family farm furnished complete with family.


Lost in this wheat field – somewhere –
and it's nobody remembers where.
But they don't care.
The dead don't care.
Not very much.

## Not a Farmer

When I turned 21 my dad took me to the tavern in town where farmers sit around and talk. Every farmer who came in would join us there at our table. Then a guy came in who wasn't a farmer but we all knew the guy. He came over and talked for a minute and then he walked away. I said to my dad, "Why didn't that guy sit at the table with us?" My dad said, "He isn't a farmer."

About that time I started hanging around with stand-up comics and people who called themselves performance poets and they got me to do shows in nightclubs where they worked.

When you do a show in a nightclub with a bunch of comics or poets you sometimes end up at some table together in a bar or an all-night restaurant, talking shop. When there wasn't much work on the farm I'd go off and recite poetry on stages, and when there was more farm work, like planting and harvest, I'd stay close to home.

The last year that I was farming, we had a friend in California who rented a little farm-ground and owned some equipment but my dad would say all the time, "He's not a real farmer." So I finally said to my dad, "How can you say that about him? He raises crops. He has equipment. He's as much a farmer as I am." My dad said to me, "You're not a real farmer either."

But I was too a farmer because every time when I filed my taxes I put under *occupation:* performance poet-slash-farmer. It's right there on the tax form.

My dad doesn't think of a farmer as a person who grows things and drives a tractor. Farming, for him, is some kind of an abstract ideal transcending the shovel in the dirt and rising like Jesus on Ascension Sunday. Like an unattainable nirvana laughing at you, "Catch me if you can, pretty boy."

Like in the age of medieval knights. A knight had to have more than shining armor. You had to be a knight on the inside. A monk or a nun had to have more than a habit or a cowl: You had to have it inside. It's like, nobody knows the meaning of *Semper Fi* the way a Marine knows the meaning of *Semper Fi*... inside. It's like, you can take the boy out of the country but you can't take the internal reality of country-ness outside of the boy's individual subjective experience... inside.

I remember the first time I had business cards made. I wanted the cards to say "poet-slash-farmer." The people at the print shop didn't ask for any verification. I could have said, "brain-surgeon-slash-rocket-scientist-slash-space-man-slash-slasher-film-actor-and-director." Nobody asked any questions. You're at the print shop and you say, "I'm a serial killer," and all they say is, "Do you want that on glossy or card stock?"

My dad said, "You're not a farmer," and I'm thinking, what do I have to do to earn his respect? I already lost thirty thousand dollars growing crops this year. Doesn't that make me a farmer?

My dad said, "When you borrow a million dollars and buy land and equipment and grow potatoes, then I'll call you a farmer." Well, I know I'll never do that. I like potatoes but what if I can't sell 'em – I don't like 'em that much. But I also know it's not about money. It's about experiencing forces that change you... inside.

I know exactly what my dad means when he talks about farming. You have to risk everything to be a real farmer: make it or break it; nowhere else to turn. Same way with doing shows. You risk everything every time you get on a stage. Tested by fire. Survival of the fittest. Are you able to be baptized with the baptism with which I am baptized? The stage connected us to each other *inside*. A fellowship of believers, hammering away at an audience like demented carpenters.

I don't know if you remember the farm crisis of the 1980s. My dad almost lost the farm back then. And he couldn't sleep at night. He was eating Pepto Bismols one after another. But the experience didn't make him want to *quit* being a farmer. The experience made him into *more* of a farmer. It was like the Universe was reaching down and saying, "Let's see what you really are." Then you have it inside – this is what you really are.

## Halfway Empty

When I left the farm to work inside an office
    I was wisened up to understand
    how good I had it back there on the farm
    with a solitude so perfect,
    so immensely peaceful silent you could hear
    the sunlight pouring down –
    the photons striking in a particle and wave
    transcending time and space.
The farm is a place where you are so alone that you
    can urinate just anywhere you want.
    Don't try that in an office parking lot.
    You'll see how quick the boss'll call you in
    for a closed-door meeting then.
Back when I left the farm it was because of money.
There's just not enough of the money.
Needed money.
And from that perspective, looking at it, I can see
    the cup was halfway empty, but
    from sitting in an office
    it appears the cup was halfway full.
So many people in an office and it's
    not that I don't like them, but they're going,
    "Do you have the time
    to double check these pages?" and

"Can you input these press releases?"
and the phone is ringing;
always someone on the phone.


But I'm still standing in the sunlight on the farm
where photons take me over time and space and
show me that the cup is halfway empty
and the cup is halfway full.


In my head I feel as if I'm halfway full of the place,
the smell of the air, the sound of the irrigation water
rolling over a check in the ditch.
I hear it right here.
In my stomach I feel as if I'm halfway empty
in the spring when I should be planting corn again
but I'm stuck at a desk at a monitor typing – gawd, and
I'm quick on a keyboard – and
I'm on the phone all the time.
It doesn't matter.
It doesn't matter at all.
It's all in the past and it's gone.


A lot of the time I wish I were
*all the way* full
of the place and I had it up to here
so I didn't have any more room for it.
I hear the hammering of iron somewhere in the distance and
I'm back in the shop on the farm.

## The Five Stages of Quitting Farming

I see a tractor working the land along the highway, and
      I say to myself,
"I can do that. I can do that. I did that."


A time or two I'd rather I didn't have any part
      of the place calling me back and
      eating inside of me
like a swather sickle chewing away at my gut;
like a noble plow tearing into the soil;
like an auger churning...
This is a Maalox moment.
I'm halfway empty and I'm halfway full and
      I'd rather be all of just one and not both.
Feet in an office and head in a field,
      rather be all of just one and not
      halfway empty and halfway full,
and it's all in the past and it's gone.

# Depression

# Guilt Feelings

Guilt feelings are a natural stage in the process of grieving over any kind of loss. I say "feelings" because there's a difference between feeling guilty and really being guilty. In the current agricultural economy it isn't reasonable to blame yourself. How could an apple grower know that China would plant millions of acres and take our foreign markets? How could a vegetable producer have anticipated that free trade would rob him of the domestic market?

It isn't rational to feel guilty about economic forces beyond your control. But you'll feel guilty, because it's in the nature of a farmer to keep trying to find a solution. American farmers have such ingenuity and optimism, they generally expect to find a way through any troubles. When you find there isn't a solution you'll say to yourself, "What did I do wrong?" and "If only I'd have done something different."

It might help to know the guilt feelings are normal. In the course of the grieving process, your mind will be coming up with things you could have done, you should have done. You'll blame yourself even if it's not your fault.

## Who Am I to Quit?

My father was a farmer: one of the first
      potato growers in the Columbia Basin Irrigation Project
      commissioned by Franklin D. Roosevelt.
Who am I to quit?
Half-a-century growing potatoes and wheat
      and apples and corn and seed crops
      and you-name-it.
Who am I to leave him?
My grandfather filed a homestead claim and
      cleared land in southern Idaho and raised
      potatoes and alfalfa and wheat and livestock.
Who am I to do anything else?
My great-grandfather emigrated from Russia
      to Washington State and grew wheat.
Who am I?
My great-great-grandfather grew wheat
      in Gluckstal, Russia.
All the way back. They were all farmers.
Who am I?

## A Real Farmer

Here's what a real farmer is:
A real farmer is one of those relentless saps
      who doesn't quit the business
      even when there's a chance to get out
like I did,
quitting while we still had a little money left;
seeing the handwriting on the balance sheet.
"Another year like this and we'll be
      too deep in debt to walk away."
A real farmer doesn't quit.

That's what a real farmer is.
And it isn't a matter of what he does,
like when a person sizes you up with a question,
      "What do you do?"
They think they got you figured out when you
      answer that "what do you do" thing.
What being a farmer is about is... it's a matter of
      what he is inside in his gut.
Not enough sense to leave, a real farmer stays
      to find a way back in;
      to work around it
while his creditors press in until — checkmate — there's
nowhere else to move.

And then a real farmer says,
"Let's set 'em up again."

If the bank won't back you
maybe the fertilizer and the seed companies
          will carry you.
And if they won't go with you
think about all those pre-approved credit cards
          coming in the mail.
And after the mortgage company forecloses
          you might even talk them into
          letting you farm it for another year
          if you'll pay the property taxes.
And go ahead. This could be the year it all pays off.
That's what a real farmer is:
Having it inside here,
the reason a real farmer can't quit being a farmer
          is that farming is what being is.
A real farmer doesn't quit
like I did.

## The Well

When my great-grandfather came to this country in 1902 he filed a homestead claim. He was the son of a farmer and his father was the son of a farmer. They were all farmers as far back as any genealogist can remember.

My great-grandfather had seven kids and his wife who was not my great-grandmother – she was his second wife. After they got established on this homestead, they hired a well-digger to dig a well.

Most of the homesteaders didn't have wells. But this well-digger came in with a steam-powered engine and all through the summer of 1908 these seven kids had to chop sagebrush out of the ground to keep the fire going in the steam engine. They worked all summer.

After the well was dug, other homesteaders in the area would bring their wagons to my great-grandfather's homestead and fill their water barrels from this well. My grandfather was the oldest son, and he didn't like people using the well. He wanted to charge money for people to use the well. But my great-grandfather said, "It's okay. They need it."

There was a drought in 1909. My grandfather used to say if they'd known how hard it was going to be in America they'd have never left Russia. They came here from Russia.

They said that in Russia the ground was so good you could grow dryland strawberries there: strawberries with no irrigation water. That might not sound impressive, but it was a hard thing to think about where they ended up in the Columbia River Basin where almost all they could grow was wheat and it was too dry for much else.

By 1911, the drought got so bad they lost the farm and had to give it up and move out. So they had everything they owned loaded onto two wagons and they were ready to leave this homestead and my grandfather said, "Let's drop some rocks down the well and fill it in."

The well was just a little pipe and if you filled it in with rocks you'd ruin it so nobody else could get any water, and my grandfather said, "Let's drop some rocks down the well." My great-grandfather said, "No, somebody else is going to need that well." So they left it alone... and they left.

## Like A Real Person

My parents sold the farm,
and this was the plan all along
because this is their retirement.
They don't have IRAs or mutual funds.
After decades here, the final act of business
      would be sell.
My parents sold the farm.
Goodbye.

But isn't it like a real person
with its temperaments and moods?
"Give me water!"
"Give me food!"
"Spend more money on me
      if you want me to treat you nice."
In the wind at night out in the orchard,
like a choir in a monastery, whispering together,
"We reach our branches to the sky,
and sink our roots into the earth."
Good advice, Granny Smith.

My parents sold the farm
and they have one month to pack the accumulation
      of five decades and move out.

Mom is boxing up the household items.
Dad is sorting through the tools and piles of iron in the shed,
and with every bolt and broken drill bit,
"Remember this?"
I remember walking through the fields all my life –
fields where I won't be welcome walking anymore.
So much packing to do before we leave.
Goodbye.


Isn't it like a real person
       the way it acts like nothing's wrong?
It doesn't even ask,
       "What are you loading the truck for?"
It doesn't ask you, "Where you gonna go?"
It doesn't... "Will you be gone long?"
Like a human being
the way it's always been a part of who we were
       and what we did.


As if we didn't just work *on* the farm:
We worked *with* the farm,
and it worked with us.


My parents sold the farm
and it's like a death in the family;
like an empty nest;
like they got divorced.
The three of them married forty-eight years.

Not as if I need it.
I'm not farming it any more.

My mom and dad, they know I tried.
But is it because of me you got divorced?
If I'd have done a better job...
Is it because of me?

The water is better on the farm
and the air is cleaner.
The soil is soft and light after the plow turns it over,
but the plow wears out.
The soil grinds it away,
from hardened steel to powder.
The land has been here longer than you,
and it'll be here when you're gone.
It won't even miss you.

My parents sold the farm
and for the first time in their lives
they have enough money to
quit working and do whatever they want.

So this is good, really.
It's a good thing.
Goodbye.

# Anger

At some point as you adjust to no longer farming you can expect to feel angry. Stoic American farmers might feel uncertain about how to handle anger.

Farmers in other countries are better at expressing anger. In France, when the government cuts price supports those French farmers riot in the streets; burn cars; break windows. The angriest thing American farmers ever did was pour milk down the drain, and one time they drove a convoy of tractors to Washington, D.C.

The important thing to remember is that anger is a natural stage of grief. This is a good time to avoid firearms. Express your anger by writing to your government representatives. After you get through the anger phase, you might be glad if you resisted the urge to write emotional letters to your relatives.

## My Parents Got a Letter

My parents got a letter
after all the packing and preparation to move away.
They got a letter from the person
      who was buying their farm.
          *"Dear John:*
          *I regret to inform you we will not be able*
          *to purchase your property*
          *per our real estate agreement."*
How do you like that?
This is sure a change in plans.
I was just getting used to the idea.
          *"As you know, we are in the fruit production*
        *business, and as you have probably been reading the*
        *fruit industry is in a shambles. We are not immune from*
        *the market forces that are deflating the value of our*
        *product. In other words, we will not be able to come up*
        *with the money for the down-payment on your property*
        *and no longer feel that expanding our orchards would*
        *do anything but lose us more money."*
My dad says to me, "The guy shook my hand.
      He shook my hand."
I don't know what to say except,
      "It's understandable, him backing out."
Dad says, "I guess a handshake

doesn't mean much anymore."

The letter:

> *"I feel terribly for you and your wife, as we know that you are looking forward to retirement. We wish things could be different but reality is setting in. We are just trying to survive to farm another year."*

That's how I feel, too.

Where is the comfortable retirement?

A farmer's land is his retirement portfolio
and the government devours that
in capital gains taxes.

> *"I thank you for all of your cooperation through our negotiations. You have been very helpful through this process. I also want to thank you for letting us use your tractor and bin trailer during our apple harvest. Since we will not be purchasing them, I would like to negotiate a lease payment for the time we used them."*

It all comes back,

and you can go back home, after all.

You can't even leave your home.

After getting all ready to say goodbye to the place.

Even wrote a stupid poem about it.

I'll be kicking dirt clods around on that place
again and again and forever.

What a change in plans.

Dad says, "I'm halfway glad.

    Moving out was too much work.

    Maybe we'll pack up and move

    to one of those assisted living places."

The letter ends,

    *"Please accept our apologies."*

# I Wish I Was Smart Like Alan Greenspan

I wish I wish
I wish I was smart like Alan Greenspan
able to see into the future... using *math*
to calculate the endless lines of cause and effect
like a Hindu lama tracing the twisted consequences
      of an economic karma;
like a Gypsy fortune-teller staring into
      a crystal ball full of dollar signs.
How I wish I had the smarts of the noble
      intellectuals on the Federal Reserve Board
when I look at my neighbors on the farms around me,
struggling to find their way out of the red ink
      when nothing –
      *nothing* you can plant –
can pay out more than it'll cost to raise it.
If it costs more to grow a crop
      than you can make when you sell it,
I mean, if you know you'll lose money
      before you even plant anything...
I wish I could see where it all ends up.
And I look at the stone cold commodities market
      and I wonder,
what does it all mean and where is it all taking us?
But I can't figure out the future any more than

an economic equation can calculate
chaotic human hearts.
I wish I was smart enough to understand
how to prepare for a future
where all the auto plants are closed and moved
to other countries, and
where all the manufacturers and the producers
and the growers have packed it in
and left the wealth of nations to the people who
produce nothing more substantial than
a cyberspace or an ethernet.
You can't hold it in your hands and you can't eat it
or wear it or safely sleep under its roof.
Every hour on the a/m radio news they play the
status of the New York Stock Exchange
but never the Chicago Board of Trade.
Every hour the doctors at the Federal Reserve Board
lean over their S&P 500 patient
with stethoscopes to their ears
as if the economic well-being of America
is based on their own indexed mutual funds,
and they never notice the crippled up
commodities market in the next bed.
I look and I wish I understood how it'll be when
nobody's producing anything anymore.
'Cause if I could really understand, maybe
I could figure out how to make money off it for myself.
I wish... I wish I was smart like Alan Greenspan.

## You Can Always Find Work

Months of job seeking,
having been forever self-employed.
No history of working for a company
        on anyone else's payroll.
No bachelor's degree.
Qualified for everything and nothing.

You can always find work in a processing plant
        or a packing shed, handling the produce
        that your former associates are still raising.
Wonder what they say about you now that
        you're just an employee.
You can find new work
although too old if you're past forty;
under-qualified without a diploma,
in spite of the experience negotiating loans,
        hiring work crews,
        managing an operation that demands
        abilities in areas too many to mention.

You can always find work in a restaurant
        peeling potatoes,
        chopping vegetables,
        washing leftover-encrusted plates

42

to make a little extra money
>while searching for a new career.

Slicing apples by the bag-full
>after growing them by the truckload.

There's an emotional demotion for you.


I met a dryland farmer who found work
>as a mortician for an extra income.

You can always do landscaping, and
>by that I mean lawn-mowing,

and there's never enough handymen around.

You can always drive tractors and change water
>for another farmer,

but if they pay the same as you paid
>your own hired men

you might not want to do that.

You might want to wash your hands
>of the whole farm industry;

get away for a while

and find work in another field altogether.


I know a guy who did two decades in the Army
>and he's getting twenty-thousand dollars
>annual retirement.

Then he got a job in the Postal Service –
>sixteen dollars an hour after just a year.

He plans to have a second retirement income
>by the time he's fifty-eight.

He sure did play that smart, it seems
      looking at the empty pockets,
      which are all that I have left.
There's no reclaiming the years you need to build
      a federal employee's pension.


You can go back to college and get a degree
      in teaching or in human services,
      or some similar area that can qualify you
to work in a career where the payroll comes
      from the taxpayers.
Remember the times you talked to a neighbor,
      sitting in pickup trucks parked side-by-side,
      about the financial security
      of a government job?
Jealous, envious: That'd be the job –
but not for you, because you're too independent
      for that sort of security.
You can always find work in sales:
      selling tractors and farm equipment,
      selling fertilizer and chemicals,
      selling vacuum cleaners,
      selling newspaper advertising.
Nobody likes to do cold calls,
      so sales jobs are always opening up.
You'll hate it, too, but it'll bring in a few dollars
      until maybe the company will shift you
      into another department.

## Anger

If you can type fast and you know how to write
you can always get a job working for a newspaper
putting press releases into the computer system, sorting
through the community events, news stories,

     births, engagements and obituaries, classified
     and legal advertisements.

Very little writing of your own,

     the days are spent repairing the
     poorly written pieces pouring in
     from other people.

Because a paper pays so little

     and demands so much,

the employee turn-over is high. So,
you can always find work
there.

## Sixteen Minutes of Hail

Wiping his cheek on his sleeve,
blowing his nose with his thumb,
I saw a farmer cry.
Big man who never cried before –
In front of me at least –
beaten down by the weather.

He'd lost his wheat.
The rain so hard it was too wet to harvest.
The rain for days until the wheat –
      it sprouted in the heads.
And he, with his uncomplaining stoicism, saying,
      "No use getting upset.
You can't do anything about the weather."

And I'm thinking,
"You can't do anything about the weather,
      farm operator,
and you can't do anything about
      the commodities market,
and you can't do anything about the government.
No use getting all Rush-beyond-Limbaugh
      irritated about it.

But I was with him on a hot and sultry day
      when ice came down from the clouds
and in just sixteen minutes –
      sixteen minutes of hail –
his entire crop of apples:
wiped out.
And he didn't speak.
His mouth hung open and his eyes got wider and –
      sixteen minutes of hail – and then
      he cried.
A man with shoulders big enough to carry seven
      hundred acres of wheat and apples
all broke up over a little frozen water.


I wanted to look away
like this was a circus freak show
and he's the naked man
      with a thousand body piercings, and
it makes you look and stare
at the man whose children's college tuition just got
      stripped away in sixteen minutes;
the man whose annual mortgage payment just got
      torn to shreds
      nine hundred sixty seconds;
the man whose wife will tell him, "We don't really
      need that new carpet and furniture.
      We don't really need that vacation trip
      you promised me."

Go ahead and cry then
you big weather target cold front from the north
      low-pressure system centering on
      seven hundred acres of wheat and apples
Congratulations.

All the neighbors saying,
      "Nice weather we're having.
      Hot enough for you?"
And you, right in the middle, get left out.

He's whispering, "No use. No use."
Turning from me to hide the red eyes.
Shoulders shaking like shocks over speed bumps.
One last breath.
One last, "No use."

And I'm thinking,
"You can't do anything about the weather."
You can't do anything about the past mistakes
      stupid things you said to your neighbors
      money you loan to your friends and relatives SAT score
      high school transcripts break a dish dent a fender not
      enough money coming in this month and she don't love
      you anymore and he don't even know you exist.
You can't do anything about your own body growing old and
      wearing out, farm operator.

And then, again he didn't speak.

Sun came out.

Clouds moved on.

And he looked at me and he said,

"No use getting upset.

You can't do anything about the weather."

## Farm Town

She's elderly,
and she says she hates being called elderly.
She says, "I'm an old, old woman
and I refuse to dye my hair.
I earned every gray hair on my head."
And she lives in a small farm town in the Northwest
where they have Victorian houses.
You can buy one for ten, fifteen,
       twenty thousand dollars,
and that's not a lot of money.

They're fixer-uppers
but you get five bedrooms, hardwood floors
       and hardwood trim around the windows.
And the reason they're so cheap is all because
if you would buy one
you would have to live there in this farm town
       where nobody wants to live.

And I'm not about to tell you where it is.
You can forget it.
I've been all over and
I've seen the little farm towns

where the people from the cities drove the prices up.
But they haven't found this one yet.
This one is mine.


In this farm town
the people there are friendly
and the grocer's is where they stop and talk
at the checkout where there's never any lines.
They need a person to be on the town council.
You'd be welcome if you bought a house in this
        farm town where I know an old, old woman.


She says my sons remind her of the kids she had
when she was younger and
she says that I remind her of her husband.
She makes me smile.
She makes me sad.
She says that every year they have a celebration.
Everyone in town shows up and brings a salad
and they have a barbecue
and they watch the fireworks.
Everyone in town:
All ninety-three of them.
They'll even feed outsiders
        if you bring your own placesetting.
They don't mind.
You're no trouble.

## The Five Stages of Quitting Farming

In this farm town
they leave their keys outside in their cars at night,
and they never lock the doors to their houses
when they sleep at night.
And they sleep at night, all night, just fine.

And I'm not about to tell you where it is.
You can forget it.
I've been all over and
I've seen the little farm towns
where the people from the cities drove the prices up.
But they haven't found this one yet.
You'll have to find it for yourself.
Don't look at me to help.
Go ask that old, old woman how to find it.
And I'll see you there.
I'll see you there.

# The Moment I Quit

I can remember the moment when I decided to quit farming, sitting at my desk, working the numbers in Excel at year's end. The income and expenses on the corn weighed in to nearly a balance and the apples, now in storage, were no different: A break-even year.

Nothing more for paying bills to support a family. A year of work and all I had was a bank account depleted by the monthly cost of living. Sitting back and staring at the monitor, having no idea of how to juggle the numbers like I did so optimistically last spring for the Farm Service Agency.

Not that I should have been surprised. The crop was contracted and the expenses estimated from the start. But with the weight slips on my desk I couldn't kid myself about expected yields anymore.

I can remember going to my mother and my father, and asking them, "If I did something else instead of renting this farm from you next year, will you be able to find another renter?" and they said they'd be okay. In fact, they seemed a bit relieved.

My father said, "Your mother and I were thinking about kicking you off the place just to make you find a different line of work."

In spite of all the times they told me I should do what I want with my life, I always felt that my father wanted me to be a farmer.

The economy is awfully cruel to make him change his mind on such a simple plan. In spite of the sense of obligation to continue the tradition of a family farm, on that day when I went to them to say I had to quit, I knew I had their blessing just as certain as Isaac blessed Jacob.

I told my dad, "Now that the harvest is in I figured out that I'll just break even for the year."

And he, knowing farming in his gut from all the years of getting kicked around by it, said, "I could have told you that last spring."

When you spend enough time at something, you get an instinct for the numbers. He didn't need Excel.

# Anger

# An Interruption May Occur

S ometimes an interruption happens and it puts an
unexpected twist in the grieving process. Sometimes
you think maybe everything is settled and you're okay
now with the way things are and then something happens to stir
up all those feelings again.

Although I'd already come to terms with the idea that
farming was over for me, an event brought everything back.

## Twenty-two Months

Twenty-two months after I told my parents
      I had to quit farming
      my dad died.
The drive home to be with my mother,
      and to be with him...
      like driving through a fog.
Like driving numb in an ocean of novocaine.
And what it is that makes no sense to me is this:
So soon?

Twenty-two months.
No more talks together in his pickup.
No more watching him with his grandkids.
No more.

Twenty-two months ago
when I told you I was giving up on
      the one thing that you lived for
did you lose the will to live,
my counselor in a pickup truck?
Were you telling me to get you to a doctor
      when you told me how easily you were
      getting tired lately?

## The Five Stages of Quitting Farming

I failed you there the way I failed to be the
      farmer you once were.


Twenty-two months you lived
      without me on that farm.
Why didn't you get your own self to that doctor?
Why didn't you ask him about your lack of energy,
you who worked so hard and did so much?
If we could have had you here just four more years
      – even three.


Twenty-two months – if I could have those back;
      the weeks; the days.
And if I'd known back then I'd have you with me
      less than two more years...
He took a shower and dressed to go to town
and then he fell asleep in his lounge chair
      in front of the TV
and never did wake up.
My neighbor said, "It's how we all want to go."
It's how he'd want to go.
Just not so soon.

## Sometimes He'd Fall Asleep

Sometimes he'd fall asleep in his pickup truck
in the sun on a cool afternoon,
and I'd check in on him
to make sure he hadn't passed away out there.
He'd open one eye from
   under the brim of his John Deere cap
to see who was standing outside.

Then I'd hop into the passenger seat
   to talk about what's up:
The little jobs;
the fields and the irrigation water;
the things we noticed around the neighbors' places.
Then we'd take a drive to check it out.

# Old

*(Written in 1991)*

He's old, and he knows he's old.
The very first time I knew my dad was old
was fifteen years ago
inside a corral
in a snowstorm.

A cow was calving and we went over
      to check how they were doing,
      the cow and the calf.
Flashlights search through the falling snow.
With all the dry ground there she dropped her calf
      in a corner where
the mud and water stood six inches deep.

Newborn calf won't last too long
      in a half-a-foot of water
      on a snowy night in January.

Flashlights on the eyes of the cow,
we both could see that one of us would have to go
      and wade into the slush;
      carry that mudball calf
      and dry him off inside the shed.
Not one word between us.

We both could see through silence
>>of the falling snow and stirring cattle.


Early days were good when dad was young
>>and he paid all the bills.
I don't know how he did it but he carried me;
>>carried me on his shoulders in the fields.
Way up on his shoulders
>>I could never see him getting older.
I saw *myself* getting stronger:
Strong enough to carry a newborn calf, at least.


Now he's old.
The very first time I knew my dad was old
was when I knew that one of us would have to go,
and without a word between us
>>I climbed over the fence and ran
>>through mud and water.
This isn't a job for a gray-haired man.
When my hair is gray I might think different.
But this was fifteen years ago.
The person my dad was then is young today,
>>and today
I don't like thinking
my dad is old.

## As My Dad Used to Say

He called me "Bud," and he's the only person
      who ever called me by that name.
Working in the shop on the farm,
      if he needed a sledge hammer he'd say,
      "Hand me that persuader over there."
If a nut was too rusty to turn off of a bolt
      he'd light the cutting torch and say,
      "I'll use the fire-wrench."
He'd call baling wire a "Mormon tool kit."
His name for the Handyman jack was
      a "widow maker"
      because the handle could flip up
      and hit you in the face,
      but we used that jack all the time.
When a repair job was finished he'd often say,
      "Good enough for who it's for,"
      which meant for ourselves.
If my rows started getting crooked
      when I planted corn, he'd say,
      "You're getting a dog leg."
If I got off-center when I was cultivating sugar
      beets and the cultivator knives
      cut the tops off of a few beet plants,
      we wouldn't know it until the tops of those plants

would wilt in the afternoon,
and he would call that "cultivator blight."
Looking at the corn, he liked to repeat the phrase,
"High as an elephant's eye
by the Fourth of July."
He claimed that if you listened carefully
on a hot summer day
you could hear the corn growing.
After listening close year after year
I'm still not sure if he was kidding.
He said if you picked up a calf
on the day it was born
and you picked it up again every day,
you could eventually pick up
a full grown bull.
When we'd go to the Farm Service Agency
to sign up for a government farm program,
he'd call it, "Bellying up to the trough."
One time when I was a kid I had the pickup truck in reverse,
driving beside the corral with the door open, and
it snagged a hay bale. The door
was dented and the hinges were sprung, and
I was sure scared when I showed him the damage.
He looked at it and all he said was,
"Did you learn anything?"
If I ever said "I wish," he'd say, "Wish in one hand
and spit in the other
and see what you get the most."

If I didn't work fast enough he'd say,

     "Grandma was slow but she was old.

     What's your excuse?"

and "Take your time but hurry up."

He repeated lyrics or media phrases, like

     Tonto's line from the Lone Ranger,

     "Get 'em up, Scout."

He seemed to only know one line from any song,

     like when he'd sing, "When you see me comin'

     you better step aside.

     A lot of men didn't and a lot of men died."

In the morning, to the tune of the Army reveille,

     "I can't get 'em up. Oh I can't get 'em up.

     Oh I can't get 'em up in the morning."

I don't even know what song the line was from, but

     he'd sing in the morning,

     "Listen to the bacon frying

     as it's sizzling in the pan."

Another song he'd sing in the morning went,

     "Lazy bones, sleepin' in the noon-day sun.

     How you gonna get your day's work done?"

He'd remember a poem on summer days,

     "Mosquito you fly high,

     mosquito you fly low,

     mosquito you fly on me,

     and you ain't gonna fly no mo'."

My son, Will, at three years old fell out of the

     pickup truck. He wasn't hurt.

Dad repeated an old phrase, "He went down
like a sack of potatoes."
William remembers that phrase to this day.
Dad liked to recite a quote that he said
went around during World War II.
Attempting an impression of FDR, he'd say,
"I don't want war
and the people don't want war,
but Eleanor wants war
so I guess we're going to have war."
He liked to rattle off the phrase,
"I kicked old Nellie in the belly in the barn."
If you stood between him and the television,
he'd say, "You make a better door
than you do a window."
He'd call a quarter "two bits," a five-dollar bill
"a five spot," and a ten-dollar bill
"a sawbuck."
I only once heard him say, after a quiet pause
in a conversation about missed opportunities and
money he'd lost in bad years,
"I love the land."
I only heard him say it once
but I knew he meant it.
He was the only person who ever called me Bud,
and nobody will ever call me
by that name again.
If they do I won't answer.

# Acceptance

I've been told that at some point the dark clouds pass and the sun comes out again. People have reassured me that at some point you'll have a sense of peace inside about the experiences you had in agriculture.

You'll even look back and remember some of it without the sadness and guilt and frustration that you had eating away inside you at one time. At some point you'll have such peace inside, you might even try getting back into farming again. You better watch out for that one.

## Where the Grass Grows Greenest

The grass sure grows green in the pasture
    around that fencepost
    where the hired man lost his leg.
He knew about augers on post-hole diggers.
An auger never cares who you are.
I don't know how anyone could get into
    that kind of trouble,
    but if anyone could he'd be the one.

The grass carried the stain for days
and the flies swarmed on the sticky dark patch
    where the hired man dug his last post-hole.
He was settled into the hospital when
    we stuck a railroad tie into the hole
    and finished his job.
The grass sure grows green there.

## I Take Walks at Night

I take walks at night under the stars and
those stars out over the farm are sure bright
where the night is darker.
I take walks at night on the farm because
it feels like a place where someone listens;
someone like the Universe;
or the Collective Consciousness; or
God. And I ask the same question
over and over, I ask, "Why is it so hard?"
Life, I mean. I'm talking about life
when I ask, "Why is it so hard?"
Just one time I got an answer.
I was all tied up inside
with knots of regret and frustration
and giving-up type knots in my gut,
and I groaned, "Why is it so hard?"
And I swear I heard a voice say,
"You're opening it from the wrong end."

# If I Can't Be a Farmer

If I can't be a farmer;
If I don't have the words inside that only a farmer can write,
I'll write poetry about political discontent
      and angry diatribes over social injustices
      committed against the downtrodden masses
      who have no voice.
I think I can find those people.
They must be someplace. You know,
      those downtrodden masses.
If I forget what farming means –
The farming my parents knew and
      that I thought I understood
      for one brief disappearing moment –
If I forget
I'll write flowery strings of adjectives about love
      and the beauty of nature and trees and swans and
      God help me if it comes to that.
      Oh man, my life has degenerated into this.
If I no longer know the technical state-of-the-art
      of agriculture as it changes and evolves
I'll write about something else. I don't know what.
Maybe I'll write Zen haikus
capturing the essence of the moment
      in a specific number of syllables

and because they're short

I can write a whole bunch.

And it'll be easy because most people are too busy

      counting syllables to notice whether I really captured

      the essence of anything.

Pretty sneaky, huh?

Maybe I'll write about my childhood

the way some academic poets write

      as if they have no other life experience,

      cloistered away in their ivy halls.

I'll write whatever I want to write

if I can't be a farmer.

I'll write erotic poetry to read late at night

      in a little metropolitan café;

      something about romance like a river ride;

      out of control emotion carrying, caressing,

      entangling, engulfing

      or whatever that stuff does.

I never had anything new to say about that sort of thing.

I should take a college class about it.

If it's all over for me with farming

      let's not dwell on it.

When are we going to quit beating this dead horse?

I'll ride the ghost of that horse all my life.

If it's over, it's over and let's move on,

and even if I still see everything

      through the same two eyes

I'll write about something else.

## Something Occurred to Me

Something occurred to me
when I was puttering with a patch of peas
    in my garden.
It occurred to me that I've become
    a backyard gardener.
Thousands of tons of corn and apples in my past
and now I'm a weed-pulling, hose-hauling,
    backyard-gardener buying Round-up
    in squirt bottles and corn seed in
    eighty-nine cent envelopes.

Something occurred to me
when I got past the humiliation. I thought about
I haven't had to water my strawberries all year.
Moving out of the Eastern Washington desert
    and into the Western Washington rain forest,
you can grow dryland strawberries here
like my great-grandfather did in Russia.
And it occurred to me,
the cranberry growers going broke
    growing cranberries
could raise raspberries here.
But it doesn't sound as good to be
    a raspberry raiser.

## The Five Stages of Quitting Farming

They can't think of anything but cranberries.
Like my dad, looking back on the year
      he lost a hundred thousand
      on a potato crop, saying
"I couldn't think of anything but planting spuds."

It occurred to me here in this rain forest,
thinking of my people and dryland strawberries,
you can raise ginseng here.
I read about a ginseng grower getting eighty
      thousand an acre, net.
It wouldn't take much to gear up for ginseng,
and you can grow it here
unlike back in the desert where I was before.

Anyway, I'm through with farming.
It's just something that occurred to me.

# Acceptance

# The Five Stages of Quitting Farming

## You Are The Light

(Written for an appearance at *The People's Poetry Gathering* in Lower
Manhattan, New York, March, 2001.)

I was thinking about New York
     on the way over here,
I was thinking, "You are the center of the art world,
and I'm from a town with a population of
     two hundred... people."

You're a city we can see from a satellite.
Your light is so bright...
     You are the light of the world.
A city sitting on eight million people cannot be hid.

I'm the voice of one crying in the wilderness.
I'm the sound of a tree falling in the forest
     without a camera crew.
You are the gateway to freedom;
Lady Liberty lifting your lamp
     beside the golden door, shouting,
"Nobody gets into America
     unless they get past me first."

I'm the sound of a field of corn growing
     on a ninety-eight degree day.
I'm the sound of a hay baler
     pounding out dairy feed
     like an all-night bass drum rehearsal
     in a second-story studio
     at a busy intersection
     of a city that never sleeps.

You're the city where somebody's always awake,
and you could get by with half as many beds
      if you had to – just trade off.
When you go out to the country
      what do you expect to see?
A reed shaking in the wind?
Looking for a guru on a mountaintop?
A shaman on a reservation?
A person of the land?
A man of the soil?
Silken sow's ear purse-like person,
Sub-suburban city slicker
metro-cultured crop cultivating
agricultural social climbing
concrete kicking tractor driving
hermit hick ascetic monk.
I'm the light of the world
and you're the light of the world.
Let your light so shine to show your world to me
and I'll show my world to you.
And I'm happy to be here in New York.

# Addenda

# The Five Stages of Quitting Farming

# Acknowledgements

"Next Year Country" appeared in *Children Remember Their Fathers*, published by gazoobi tales, Everett, Washington, 2000.

"Cemetery" appeared in *Vox Populi 1999 Seattle Poetry Festival Anthology*, Eleventh Hour Productions, Seattle, Washington, 1999.

"Farm Town" appeared in *Willow Springs*, Eastern Washington University, Cheney, Washington, January 1999.

An earlier version of "Where the Grass Grows Greenest" appeared in *Revival: Spoken Word from Lollapalooza 94*, Manic D Press, San Francisco, California, 1995

Thanks to Nancy Butterfield, Ramey Holsman, Sheryl Sirotnik and Clarice Keegan for their help, and to Bitsy Bidwell and the Washington State Arts Commission for always being available with advice and encouragement. Thank you, Susan Carney, for your endless care and support.